HELVETIQ publishing has received a structural grant from the
Swiss Federal Office of Culture for the years 2021–2025.

Vigdís
A book about the world's first female president

Copyright © Rán Flygenring, 2019 (text and illustrations)
Title of the original Icelandic edition: Vigdís: Bókin um fyrsta konuforsetann
First published in Icelandic by Angústúra.
Published in the English language by arrangement with
Reykjavik Literary Agency, Iceland, www.rla.is

Author and illustrator: Rán Flygenring
Typesetting and layout: Chloé Châtelain, Ewelina Proczko
Translator: Jonas Moody
Proofreader: Sonia Curtis

ISBN: 978-3-03964-041-6

First North American Edition: 2024
Deposit copy in the Library of Congress: 2024
Printed in China

helvetiq.com

MIX
Paper from
responsible sources
FSC® C167893

RÁN FLYGENRING • TRANSLATED BY JONAS MOODY

Vigdís

A BOOK ABOUT THE WORLD'S FIRST FEMALE PRESIDENT

When I grow up I
want to be a writer.

So far I have written
one book, which is called
THE MONSTER THAT
WENT TO EGYPT.

It's not actually done
all the way because I got
an idea for a new book!

A book about
THE FIRST WOMAN IN
THE WORLD WHO WAS
ELECTED PRESIDENT.

Mom doesn't know much about presidents.

But she also says don't let the world stop you from following your dreams.

Vigdís Finnbogadóttir was once the president of Iceland. Now she lives in a house in Reykjavík, not so far from my house! It has been her home for more than fifty years and she told me that sometimes she wonders what the walls would say if they could talk...

Everything in her house has a story to tell.

When Vigdís was two, her brother Þorvaldur was born. He was named after their grandfather, but everyone called him Bói.

See how tight I'm holding his hand? I thought he was so little and dear, and I wanted to keep him safe.

When Vigdís and Bói were kids, Iceland didn't have a president. Back then, the king of Denmark ruled over Iceland too.

Bói and Vigdís grew up in Reykjavík. Even though it's Iceland's capital, back then it wasn't much of a city. Just a small town with muddy streets, corner shops and farms. Their house was near a farm called Ásvellir and sometimes the sheep would escape and come eat all the garden flowers!

In the autumn, the family would pick berries on the mountainsides, and on Sundays they went for walks along the shore.

There were no TV and phones, so they read a lot of books.

But on Thursdays, Vigdís and Bói got to listen to a radio play before bed.

After school, Vigdís sometimes got to help her mom run errands around town.

Their favorite food was fishcakes and ketchup!

World War II broke out when Vigdís was ten. British soldiers came to stay in Iceland and went around Reykjavík with guns and trucks.

That's when Vigdís and Bói were sent to the countryside, because it was thought to be safer than the city.

Vigdís said she loved country life, but she always dreamt of being a sea captain and sailing around the world. However, when she told people this, she was just given a pat on her head and told that she could never do that because she was a girl!!

WHAT?!!

I couldn't believe it.

When Vigdís moved back to Iceland after many years away, she taught Icelandic people how to speak French, both in high schools and on national TV.

She also worked as a tour guide showing people around Iceland's mountains and fjords.

Then she adopted her daughter, Ástríður. Vigdís became the first single woman in Iceland to adopt a child.

Next Vigdís told me about her BIGGEST PASSION...

... the THEATER! Vigdís has probably seen more than a THOUSAND plays because she managed a theater for many years.

She says that in the theater you can learn a lot about people.

One day in 1975 when Vigdís was working in the theater, there was a strike.
All over the country, women stopped working, came out into the streets and demanded the same opportunities and rights as men.

Vigdís and the other women who worked in the theater took part.

Five years later, it was time for Icelanders to choose a new president, and three men announced they were running.

But since the women's strike, many people started to think differently. They wanted a woman to run too!

One day the paper ran a letter from a reader:

Many knew Vigdis from TV and the theater,
but even she thought the suggestion
of her as president was ridiculous!
Until then it had been a job reserved
for accomplished, old men...
She had no interest in running!

But the letter in the paper was just the beginning. Vigdis got calls, letters and visits from friends and acquaintances all urging her to run!

Vigdis herself, however, was still not behind the idea.

Then one day Vigdís received a TELEGRAM from a crew of fishermen in the Westfjords:

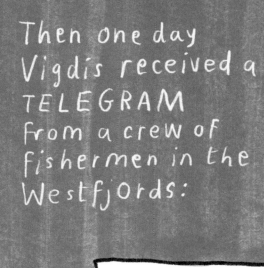

TELEGRAM

FROM: Ísafjörður   30.JAN.1980
                          TIME: 13:48

To: Vigdís Finnbogadóttir

WE, THE UNDERSIGNED,

URGE YOU TO ANNOUNCE

YOUR CANDIDACY FOR PRESIDENT

OF ICELAND.

BEST REGARDS,

THE CREW OF GUÐBJARTUR ÍS

Since a whole boatload of fishermen she didn't even know wanted this landlubber for president, she figured it was time to really consider it.

Soon Vigdís was made Iceland's president at a big ceremony called an INAUGURATION.

Up until then, all democratically elected presidents of the world were, and always had been, men.

Vigdís and Ástríður moved to Bessastaðir.
That's where the president of Iceland lives.

Bessastaðir is on ÁLFTANES, which means
"SWAN PENINSULA."

Vigdís liked to offer her guests her signature Bessastaðir cookies—they are very tasty!

At Bessastadir, Vigdís welcomed guests, hosted receptions, gave speeches and awards and met with politicians. But as the head of state she also got to travel a lot.

Vigdís visited kings and queens in countries far away.

And hosted them when they visited Iceland.

Her most precious moments were when she was asked to visit the countryside. Then she would bring three birch saplings along to plant in the ground with the help of the local kids.

One for all the girls,
One for all the boys
and one for all the children
yet to be born!

THE AUTHOR WOULD LIKE TO THANK VIGDÍS HERSELF & HER DAUGHTER ÁSTRÍDUR. THEIR SUPPORT AND COOPERATION WERE ESSENTIAL IN BRINGING THIS BOOK TO LIFE. ALSO MANY THANKS TO EDDA HAFSTEINSDÓTTIR FOR THE IDEA.